STARTING
DRAWING

Anna Claybourne

Designed by Lindy Dark
Edited by Fiona Watt
Illustrated by Terry Burton and Lindy Dark
Photographs by Howard Allman
Art consultant: Gill Figg

Series editor: Cheryl Evans

Contents

Things you need

You don't need much to start drawing. You can draw with any pencil, pen, crayon or chalk on all different kinds of paper. These two pages show you some of the things that will be useful for doing the projects in this book.

Pencils

A pencil is the easiest thing to draw with, and pencils are cheap and easy to find. Pencil leads can be harder or softer. They make different kinds of marks.

110 2B

Look on the side of the pencil for the label showing the hardness of the lead.

H stands for hard and B stands for black. Black pencils are softer. A 6B is a very soft pencil, which you can smudge easily. H pencils are harder and make fainter lines. An HB pencil is in the middle.

2H

HB

2B

6B

The higher the number, the softer or harder the pencil.

Paper

Art and craft stores sell many different kinds of paper in all shades and sizes. Look for paper with interesting textures, such as rough, smooth and shiny.

Smooth white artists' paper often comes in a pad. You can buy different sizes.

Sugar paper has a rough surface and comes in different shades.

Pens and crayons

You can do bright drawings with pencils, crayons, felt-tip pens, chalks or pastels.

Bright pencils are good for detailed drawings and delicate shades.

Pastels or chalks can be smudged and blended together with your finger.

Crayons are bright and bold.

Felt-tip pens are good for filling in spaces.

You can draw on cardboard too. Try the inside of a cereal box.

Some of the projects in this book use tracing paper.

Paper comes in lots of bright shades.

Tissue paper

Extra things

As well as drawing, this book has some exciting projects for you to do. You will need scissors, paper glue, tape and a pencil sharpener. You also need a large, flat table or other space to work on.

Charcoal

Charcoal makes a mark like a very soft, black pencil. It is made from burned twigs. Artists often use it for sketching pictures. You can buy it from art and craft stores.

To smudge charcoal, draw on paper and gently rub the marks with your finger.

Charcoal also comes in pencils.

Charcoal is very messy, so cover pictures with another piece of paper before you put them away.

Other ways to draw

You don't have to use only pens and pencils. Try out some more unusual tools.

Try drawing with a brush and ink or thin paint.

If you go to a sandy beach, you can do huge drawings in the sand with a stick or your finger.

Use a cotton bud and paint to do a simple picture.

Try doing a drawing with a twig dipped in paint or ink.

Making marks

You can use pencils, crayons and other drawing tools to make lots of different marks and patterns.

Lines

Lines can be straight or curly, thick or thin, long or short. How many different kinds of lines can you make?

Can you draw a straight line without a ruler?

Try holding a pencil on its side and drawing with the side of the lead.

You can use long lines to make shapes.

Lots of short lines close together can look like fur or grass.

Sharp or hard pencils make thin lines.

Use a blunter or softer pencil for thicker lines.

With soft pencils, chalks or pastels, you can smudge lines with your finger to make them softer.

Dots and spots

Drawing lots of little dots with the tip of a pencil or pen is called pointillism (say *pwant*-ill-ism). You can use it to fill in big spaces.

Try a mixture of dots in different shades. From farther away, the shades blend together.

Rubbing patterns

Making rubbings is a good way to make marks. Find things that have rough patterns, or textures, on them, such as wooden things, keys or leaves.

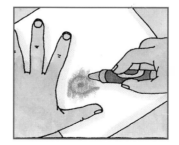

To make a rubbing, hold a piece of paper still over the thing and rub up and down over it with a crayon or soft pencil.

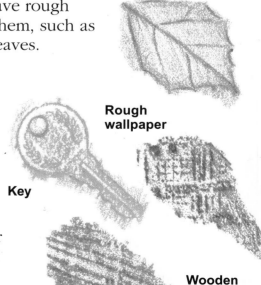

Leaf

Rough wallpaper

Key

Wooden table

Big-leaved tree picture

You can use different kinds of drawing marks to make whole pictures.

You will need:
Pencils, crayons or pastels
Thin, smooth paper in different shades
Rough brown or green paper or cardboard
Scissors and glue
Small leaves

1

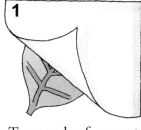

Turn a leaf over to show the ridges on the back. Lay some white paper on top and hold it still.

2

Using the edge of a pencil or crayon, rub gently up and down on the paper all over the leaf.

3

Make leaves of different shades and sizes.

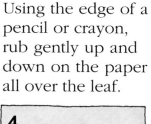

Carefully cut around the outline of the leaf. Make more leaves in the same way.

4

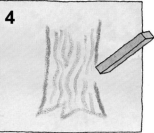

For a tree trunk, draw thick, wavy green and brown lines on the rough paper or cardboard.

5

Overlap the leaves.

Cut the trunk out and glue it onto a large piece of paper. Then glue the leaves around the top.

You could make rubbings from other things, and then cut out leaf shapes from them.

You could show a leaf falling off the tree.

Draw short green lines to make grass.

Seeing shapes

Everything you can see is made up of shapes. These pages show you how to look for shapes and draw outlines.

Air drawing

Before you draw something, look at its shape carefully. Close one eye, reach out, and "draw" around the object in the air with your finger. This is called air drawing. It helps you see what shape things are.

Some things, such as a bottle, have a simple shape.

Some things have a complicated shape, like this leafy plant.

Drawing outlines

1

Start with a simple shape.

Choose something to draw. Place it a short distance away from you. Look carefully at its shape.

2

Try air drawing the thing (see above) to help you see exactly what shape it is.

3

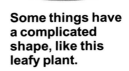

Now use a pencil to draw the outline on your paper. Don't draw the details inside the shape.

Try something with a more complicated outline.

4

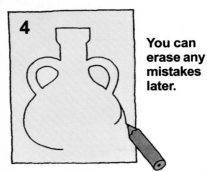

You can erase any mistakes later.

If it looks wrong, just draw a new line where you want it and leave the old one there.

Look around for things that have interesting shapes.

Shape collage

A collage is a picture made of lots of shapes glued onto paper. You can make a collage of the different shapes you have drawn.

You will need:
A pencil
Paper of different shades, textures and thicknesses
Scissors and glue

Can you tell what all these shapes are?

You can make the shapes overlap.

Tissue paper

Pattern of dots made with a felt-tip pen

Shiny paper

1

Choose a collection of things to draw. You could just use things from the kitchen, for example.

2

Using a pencil, draw outlines of all the things on different kinds of paper.

3

If you like, you could add dots, lines or other patterns, like the ones on page 4, to your shapes.

4

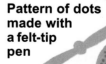

Carefully cut out the shapes and arrange them on a large piece of paper. Glue them down.

Taking a line for a walk

Most things are made up of lots of shapes. Here's an interesting way to put all the shapes together. You move smoothly from one part of your picture to another without taking your pen off the paper. This is called taking a line for a walk.

You will need:
A felt-tip pen and some paper
Something to draw, such as a shoe, a flower or a person

Start drawing

1

You could use a photograph.

Begin by looking carefully at the thing you are going to draw. What shapes can you see?

2

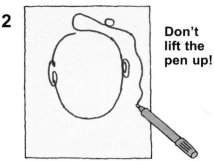

Don't lift the pen up!

Put your pen on the paper to start your drawing. It is easiest to start with the outline of your picture.

3

Make your line curve and twist to include the main shapes. You don't have to draw every detail.

You can go over the same line twice.

You may have to do a line where you can't really see one. In this picture, for example, there is a line from the hair to the eyebrow.

Use your line to do squiggles, shading in, or other patterns along the way.

Abstract line walk

An abstract drawing is a drawing that isn't a picture of anything. Sometimes it's just lots of shapes. You can make an abstract drawing by taking a line for a walk all over a piece of paper.

Draw a long line that curves, twists, zigzags or crosses over itself to make lots of patterns. Fill in the spaces in different shades.

You could fill in the spaces with patterns (see page 4).

Try an abstract line walk using just straight lines.

Mounting

Mounting a picture on a bright background gives it a border, which looks good when you display your work.

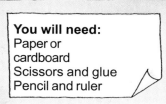

You will need:
Paper or cardboard
Scissors and glue
Pencil and ruler

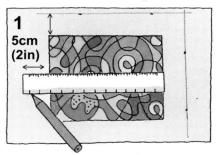

1
5cm (2in)

Measure a piece of paper or cardboard 5cm (2in) wider and 5cm (2in) taller than the picture on each side.

2

Cut out the cardboard or paper mount and glue your picture neatly in the middle of it.

Shading and blending

Shading means filling in the dark and light areas in your drawings. It makes things look solid and real. The darkness or lightness of a mark is called the tone. Harder and softer pencils (see page 2) make different tones.

Dark to light

1 Sharpen the pencil if it gets blunt.

To make a very dark tone, press hard with your pencil. Go over the same part again and again.

2

Try to keep the tone even.

To make lighter tones, hold the pencil on its side, press gently, and shade back and forth.

3

Try different shades using bright pencils.

Try changing tone gradually along in a strip on the paper. Press less and less hard as you go.

Find out how to draw these zooming rockets below.

Zooming rockets

Soft drawing tools like charcoal and pastels are easy to smudge and blend. Use them to draw a whoosh of rocket flames.

You will need:
A large piece of paper
Felt-tip pens or crayons
Pastels, chalks or charcoal

1 You could draw the rockets with felt-tips or crayons.

Draw some flying rockets. Shade them in if you want to.

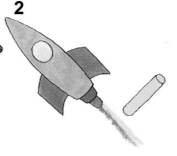

2

Draw thick charcoal or pastel lines coming from the rockets.

3 Use a quick, sweeping movement.

Use a finger to rub the flames away from the rocket.

A shaded drawing

Choose something round and simple to draw, like a ball or some fruit.

You will need:
White paper
Whatever you want to draw with, such as a pencil, charcoal or pastels
A spotlight

1

Place your object under the light. Switch off any other lights and close the curtains if possible.

2

Highlight

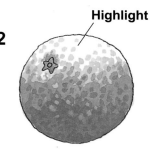

Look at the dark and light parts. The brightest part, where the light reflects, is called the highlight.

3

Try moving the light around to see how the dark and light parts change. Does the highlight move?

4

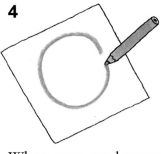

When you are happy with how the object looks, start drawing. Begin with the outline of the shape.

5

Shade in the darker parts of the drawing first, then the lighter ones. For a highlight, leave white paper.

Charcoal drawing

Pastel drawing

Try drawing the same thing using different tools or shades.

Lighter area

The different tones in something show its shape.

The highlight is in the middle of this orange.

Dark area

11

Magic cubes

There is a simple secret to drawing a cube. Once you know it, you can use cubes in lots of different ways to make pictures.

1

Start by drawing a square on a piece of paper with a pencil. This will be the front of your cube.

2

Now draw another square that is slightly smaller. Make it overlap the first square, like this.

3

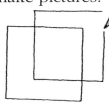

a

b

Now join the corners of the squares with lines (shown in blue). You have drawn a see-through cube.

4

To make the cube look solid, erase the three lines inside the cube (shown here in red).

Draw ribbons and bright patterns for a present.

Add a screen and buttons to make a television.

What can a cube be?

A cube can be a box, or it can be all kinds of other things. Just add details.

For a fishtank, draw a see-through cube. Add some water and fish.

You can make long boxes, or cuboids, the same way.

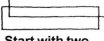

Start with two oblong shapes.

Join the corners together.

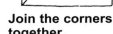

For a bus or train, draw a long oblong box. Add wheels and windows.

Light and shade

When light shines at a cube, the side nearest the light looks brightest. The other sides are in the shade, so they look darker. Try shading in your cubes like this.

Imagine a light shining from the right.

This side would be the lightest.

This side would be the darkest, if you could see it.

The other sides would be a medium shade.

Imagine a light on the left of a cube.

This side would be very dark.

You can't see the bright side.

These sides would be a medium shade.

Can you shade a cube with the light coming from other sides?

Cube robot

You can create a robot using cube and box shapes. Decorate it with eyes, feelers, controls, flashing lights, wheels or other robot parts.

You will need:
A large piece of paper
A pencil
Felt-tip pens, wax crayons or pencil crayons for shading in

1

Erase any lines you don't want as you go.

Draw big cube shapes one above the other for the robot's head, body and base.

2

Join the three parts of the robot together with wiggly wires, using a felt-tip pen or crayon.

3

Add arms, eyes, buttons, dials and any other parts you like.

4

Imagine the light is in the same place for each cube.

Shade in the cubes in different tones so that they look solid.

This side of the robot is turned away from you, so you can't see as much of the arm and ear.

This side of the robot looks nearer to you.

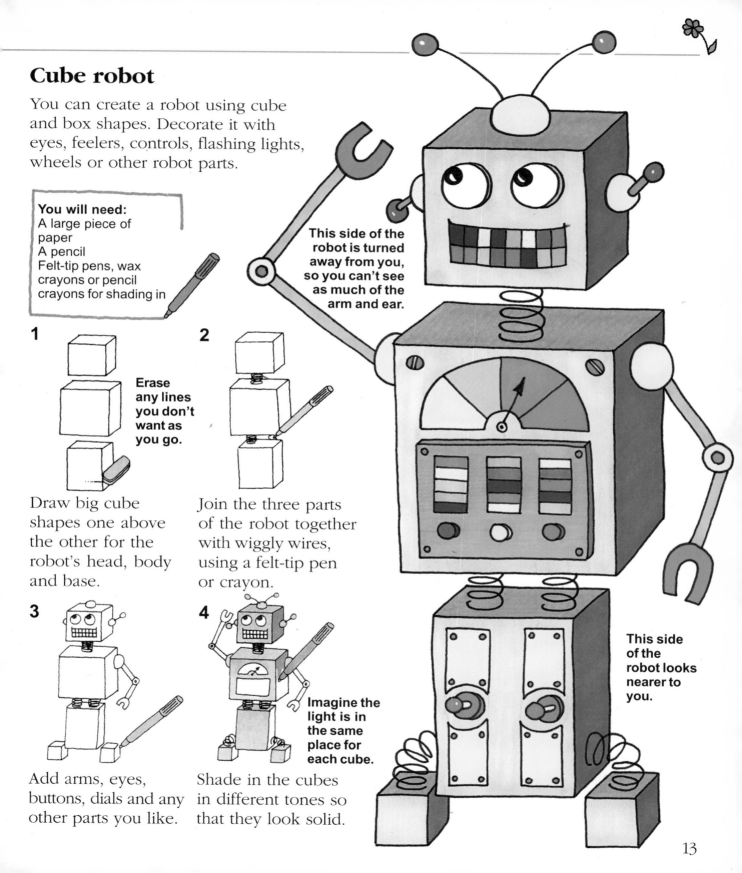

13

Near and far

Things that are near to you look much bigger than things that are far away. When you are doing a drawing, you can make some of the things in it look nearer to you by drawing them larger. To see for yourself how near things look bigger than faraway things, try the experiment below.

Foreground and background

The word foreground is used to describe things that look very near in a picture. Things that are far away are in the background.

In this picture, the ducks are in the foreground and the trees are in the background.

See for yourself

1

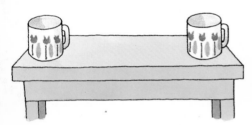

Find two things that are about the same size as each other. Place them far apart on a table, like this.

2

Stand at one end of the table. Bend down so that your eyes are level with the two things. Cover one eye.

3

Look at the two things carefully. Do they look different sizes? You could try drawing them.

Near and far landscape picture

Make a picture showing near and faraway things, using tracing paper. A landscape or outdoor picture works best.

You will need:
2 sheets of tracing paper
1 sheet of white paper the same size as the tracing paper
Felt-tips or crayons
Clear tape

1

Draw near the top of the paper.

Start by drawing the background on the white paper. Draw some hills, sky and small trees.

2

Lay a piece of tracing paper neatly over the picture. Fasten them together at the top with tape.

The three layers make it seem as if you are looking into the distance.

The tracing paper makes the faraway things look fainter, as they do in real life.

Make the nearer trees bigger than the faraway ones.

Draw some more things on the tracing paper. Make these things bigger so that they look nearer.

Now lay the second sheet of tracing paper over the drawing. Fasten it to the drawing at the top.

On the top sheet, draw the things in the foreground. These should be the biggest things in the picture.

15

Light on dark

In the dark, lights from buildings, machines and fires glow. Sometimes you can't even see the shapes of things, only the lights shining from them. Here are some ways to draw lights at night. Try using black, dark blue or purple paper and bright pastels or chalks.

Light effects

Streetlights glow like this.

You don't need to draw the outline of the building.

For a glowing light, draw a dot or square. Rub it with a finger to make it look as if it is glowing.

Draw rows of windows with a yellow chalk on black paper. They look like a skyscraper at night.

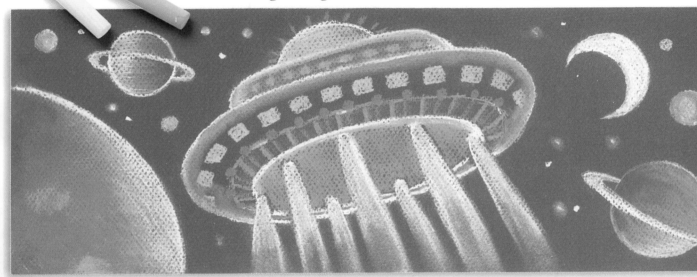

The sky at night

Using pastels or chalks, try drawing a space scene with planets and brightly lit-up spacecraft. Add stars and moons for a night sky.

You will need:
A big, long piece of black or dark blue paper
Pastels or chalks in different shades

1

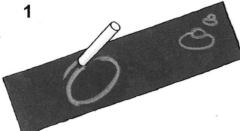

For spacecraft, draw large oval, sausage or rocket shapes on the paper.

2 Rub the lights to make them glow.

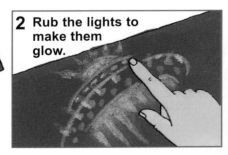

Add rows of windows, glowing lights or light beams to the spacecraft.

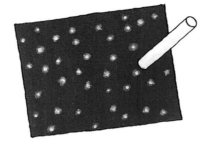

A lighthouse or a car's headlights send out beams.

Draw spots of light in yellow pastel or chalk. Rub away from the spot to make a light beam.

For stars at night, do lots of tiny white dots. Lots of yellow dots look like the lights of a town or city.

Scratch drawings

To make drawings like these, cover a piece of giftwrap or a page from a magazine with thick, black crayon.

Use a spoon or paintbrush handle to scratch a picture. The bright paper will show through the black crayon.

Try drawing fireworks or a city.

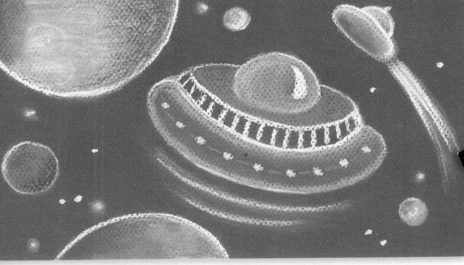

3

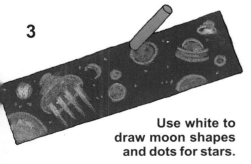

Use white to draw moon shapes and dots for stars.

For planets, draw circles and shade them in. You could add spots or patterns.

4

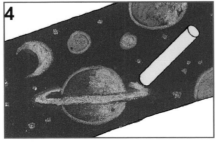

For a ring around a planet, draw a long oval, half in front of the planet and half behind.

Fantastic feet

Drawing people from real life is called life drawing. Drawing a whole person can be hard, but you could try just drawing your feet, to see what it's like.

You will need:
Plain white paper
A board or large book to rest on
A pencil, charcoal, or whatever you want to draw with
Two chairs (one to sit on, one to rest your feet on)

Feet from life

1

Hold your paper on your lap.

Sit with your feet resting on a chair. Make sure you are comfortable, so you won't have to move around.

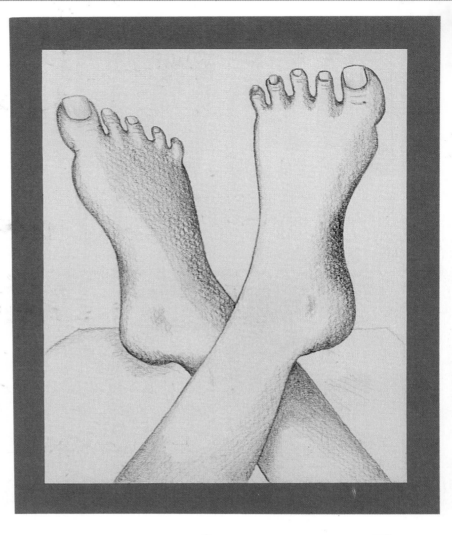

2

Start with the outline. Look carefully at the shapes you can see. You could try "air drawing" (see page 6) first.

3

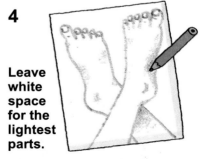

Add details of any other shapes and lines you can see, such as toenails, freckles or tiny wrinkles.

4

Leave white space for the lightest parts.

Can you see darker and lighter areas on your feet? See if you can shade them in on your drawing.

Still life shoes

Drawing things that do not move is called still life. It's easiest if you start with just one thing. Try drawing a still life of one of your shoes.

1

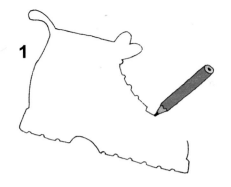

Draw the outline of the shoe. Try to include all the details around the outline, like laces and bumpy soles.

2

Does the shoe have a label or name on it?

Show the stitching and seams.

Add details such as buckles, laces, stitching or patterns. Shade in or decorate the shoe with pens or crayons.

If you can see inside the shoe, draw that part too.

To cut out a hole, poke your scissors through first.

Shoe bookmarks

Cut out the hard parts, like laces, at the end.

Draw a shoe about 10cm (4in) long on thin cardboard. Carefully cut it out to make a bookmark.

To make the bookmarks last longer, you could cover them with book-covering plastic.

Different styles

You don't always have to draw in the same way. Artists often have their own way of drawing, or style, which they like to use. Here are some different styles of drawing for you to try.

Collage

Try mixing collage (see page 7) with drawing to make pictures.

You will need:
Scissors
Glue stick
A thick felt-tip pen
Paper in different shades

1

The shapes don't have to be exactly right.

Cut simple petal shapes out of bright paper. Glue them down to make a flower shape.

2

Use simple, bold lines.

With a thick pen, draw the shape of the flower over the top of the paper pieces.

Black and white

You can do bold, striking pictures using just a black pen.

Try flowers with bold patterns, stripes and spots.

Shade part of a flower with black lines drawn close together. This is called hatching.

For darker shading draw two sets of lines that cross over each other. This is called cross-hatching.

Stained glass window

Stained glass is often used in church windows. It is made of bright pieces of glass fitted together like a jigsaw.

1

First, use a thick black felt-tip pen to draw a flower shape on a piece of paper.

2

Use bright, strong shades.

Draw curved lines across parts of the picture to divide it into smaller spaces. Shade them in.

Geometric

Shapes like triangles, circles and rectangles are geometric shapes. You can use them to make pictures.

You will need:
Felt-tip pens or pencil crayons
A coin to draw around
Plain paper
A ruler

For a flower with diamond petals, do a circle first. Draw six lines evenly spaced around the circle.

Use a ruler if you want.

Add a triangle shape on each side of each line to make the diamond petals. Then shade them in.

Make sure all the circles fit together closely.

For a flower made of circles, draw around a coin. Put one circle in the middle and the rest around it.

Try drawing a bunch of flowers in different styles.

You can use any style for the ribbon.

21

Cartoons

Cartoons are simple, funny drawings that often tell a story. Here are some ways to show different moods and feelings on cartoon faces.

Here's an ordinary cartoon face.

Different kinds of eyebrows, mixed with mouth shapes, change the mood on a cartoon face.

V-shaped eyebrows with a straight mouth look very angry.

The mouth is very important. It can make faces look sad, happy or surprised.

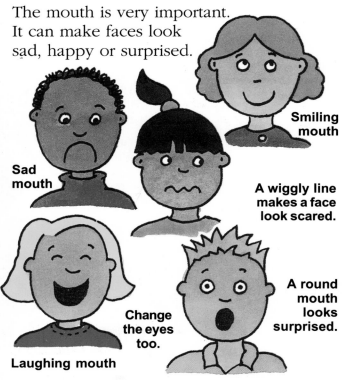

Sad mouth

Smiling mouth

A wiggly line makes a face look scared.

Change the eyes too.

Laughing mouth

A round mouth looks surprised.

Try sloping eyebrows with a sad mouth.

V-shaped eyebrows and a smiley mouth look naughty.

Try adding special effects like these to show what is happening.

Add drops of sweat for a very hot, tired person.

Add crossed eyes.

Stars or a swirly cloud around the head make a person look dizzy.

Moving bodies

Here's how to add bodies to your cartoon faces.

Erase the stick body later.

Draw a stick body, then add clothes and shoes on top.

Always draw the stick body first, then add clothes.

For a running person, show legs and arms bent like this.

Different clothes show different jobs or hobbies.

For jumping, put the arms behind the body and the legs in front.

What other things can you make stick people do?

Cartoon animals

For cartoon animals, think about the main shapes that help you recognize an animal. For example, a cat has big ears and whiskers.

Draw funny eyebrows to give the cat a mood.

Draw the mouth like a big "w."

Sometimes cartoons make animals look like people. Try a cat's face with human clothes.

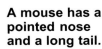

A pig is fat with a round snout and curly tail.

A mouse has a pointed nose and a long tail.

Here are some more cartoon animals to try. Give them funny cartoon faces to show different moods.

Jungle scene

You can also draw cartoon scenes, like this cartoon jungle. Remember, you can put anything you like in a cartoon, even if it wouldn't happen in real life.

A hippo has a fat body with stumpy legs and a long, bumpy head.

A giraffe has a long neck and legs.

A monkey has a big nose, big ears and a long tail.

For jungle leaves, draw long triangle shapes.

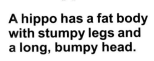

Tiger

Mane

Birds have egg-shaped bodies. Their necks can be long or short.

A crocodile has a long lumpy body.

This lion has a triangle head and a big furry mane.

Draw big, bright jungle flowers.

A snake is a wiggly shape with a round head.

23

Movement, speed and sound

Here are some tricks for making your cartoons look as if they are moving, and for showing noises and exciting actions.

Zoom lines

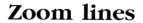

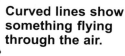

Curved lines show something flying through the air.

Draw a few straight lines behind something to show it speeding along.

For something really fast, add a cloud of dust around the lines, like this.

Draw lines on both sides of something to show it wiggling from side to side.

Splat! Boom!

In cartoons, you can show noises by drawing a word with a shape around it. Try words like Kapow! Boom! Boinggg! Splash! and Splat!

SPLAT!

Draw a puddle shape and water drops for a wet, sticky splat.

Big zigzags around a word show a loud noise or explosion.

BOOM!

Use bright red and yellow for an explosion.

KAPOW!

Draw a big flash like this to show a loud bang or crash.

The flash is made up of a circle of U shapes.

Speech bubbles

HEY! COME BACK!

HEY! COME BACK!

Write words in clear letters near the cartoon's head.

Draw an oval bubble around the words, with a small pointer.

YUM YUM!

Draw a trail of smaller bubbles leading to the thinker.

To show thoughts, do the words in a cloud-shaped bubble.

MEET ME AT HQ...

Do zigzag bubbles for a telephone or loudspeaker sound.

Animated flick book

Animated pictures look as if they are moving when you see them quickly one after another. This page shows you how to make a flick book showing a flower opening. Flick through the pictures in the top corner of this book to see how it works.

Flick this book like this.

You will need:
A small notebook with plenty of pages
Pens or pencils
Scissors and glue

1

Leave some space around the flower. **Use this edge.**

On the first page of the book, draw a small flower like this.

2

Put the flower in the same place.

On the next page, draw a slightly bigger flower.

3

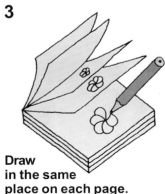

Draw in the same place on each page.

Gradually make the flower petals grow bigger and bigger.

4

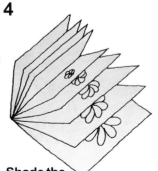

Shade the flower in, if you like.

Make the flower open out until it is as big as it can be.

When you have finished, flick through the book like this to watch the animated cartoon.

You could draw a cover picture for your flick book on a piece of paper, and glue it to the front.

More ideas

Here are some more animation ideas. Do each picture on a new page. (You will need to do more pictures than are shown here.)

Make this man walk along the page until he slips.

Make the bird fly across the page.

Make the frog jump up and down.

25

Portraits

A portrait is a drawing of a person. Artists usually draw portraits from real life, but you can copy from a photograph. You could even do a portrait of yourself, called a self-portrait, by sitting in front of a mirror.

Faces and features

Parts of people's faces, like eyes, noses and mouths, are called features. Look at how people's features are arranged on their faces. It helps if you think of the head as an oval with four parts.

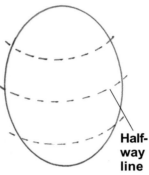

Half-way line

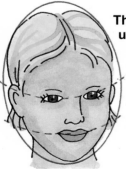

Most people's eyes are about halfway down their head.

The ears are usually level with the eyes.

The nose and mouth are just under the eyes, about three-quarters of the way down.

Hair usually fills up the top quarter of the head and is longer at the sides.

Drawing a portrait

The person you draw is called the sitter. Make sure she is comfortable. She will have to sit still for about 20 minutes.

You will need:
A piece of paper
Pencils
Something to rest on, like a large book
An eraser

1

You can erase any wrong lines later.

Lightly draw the main shapes. Most portraits show just the head and shoulders.

2

Use the shapes you have drawn to help you draw a stronger, more careful outline.

3

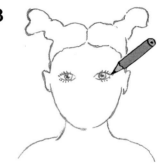

How big are your sitter's eyes, and where are they? Draw them next.

4

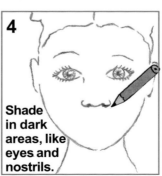

Shade in dark areas, like eyes and nostrils.

Add eyebrows and work on down the face. Look at the nose and draw that next.

5

Are there lines from the nose to the mouth?

Now draw the mouth, and any other things, like glasses or earrings.

6

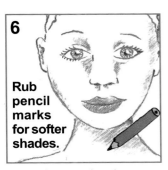

Rub pencil marks for softer shades.

Are there shadows under the chin or around the eyes or nose? Shade them in.

7

Use lines that follow the way the hair grows.

Draw in the sitter's hair and clothes. Try to copy any patterns like stripes or spots.

Stand-up mount

Here's how to make a stand-up mount to display your portraits. First, mount the portrait on cardboard, as shown on page 9.

You will need:
Cardboard
A pencil and ruler
Scissors and tape
Glue

Try making a mini-portrait.

You could draw a background too.

You could decorate the frame with felt-tip pens.

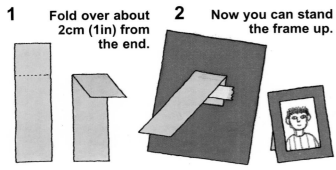

1 **Fold over about 2cm (1in) from the end.**

Cut a piece of cardboard that is smaller than your mount. Fold the end over.

2 **Now you can stand the frame up.**

Tape the folded-over part to the back of your frame, about halfway up.

Portraits long ago

Before photographs were invented, rich people often used to pay to have their portraits drawn or painted.

Design and make a mask

Sometimes it's easier to make things if you think about what you want them to look like and draw them first. This is called designing. These pages show you how to design a mask on paper, and then make it using cardboard.

Designing

1

A made-up mask?

An animal mask?

First, decide what kind of mask you want to make. Try drawing some of your ideas on paper.

2

What shape should it be?

Could you glue things onto it?

Think about how you could make the mask look the way you want it to. There are some ideas below.

3

Keep trying out ideas until you decide on a design you want. Now you can make a pattern for a mask.

4

Leave lots of space around the oval.

On a new piece of paper, draw an oval base shape about 20cm (8in) tall and 15cm (6in) wide.

5

Change and correct it as much as you like.

Now draw the shape you want your mask to be, around the base shape. This is your mask pattern.

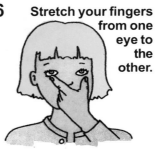

6

Stretch your fingers from one eye to the other.

You will need to see out of eyes in the mask. Use your hand to measure how far apart your eyes are.

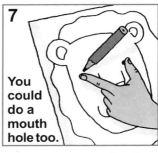

7

You could do a mouth hole too.

Use your stretched fingers to mark two eye spots halfway up the oval. Draw eye holes around them.

Design ideas

Think about ways to make your masks look exciting.

How could you make a furry animal mask?

You could glue on pieces of yarn or wool.

Spiky edges look like fur.

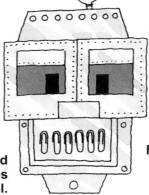

What would make it look like a robot?

Foil or silver paper looks like metal.

You could glue on small metal things, such as paper clips.

What could you do to make it look like a person?

You could cut a hat shape out of cloth.

Moustache and beard made of crepe paper.

Making your mask

Now you can use your design to help you make the finished mask out of cardboard.

You will need:
Thin cardboard
Pencil, scissors, tape
Pens or crayons
Glue and things to glue to the mask

1

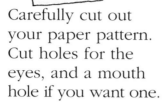

Carefully cut out your paper pattern. Cut holes for the eyes, and a mouth hole if you want one.

2

Draw any holes too.

Lay the paper design on the cardboard. Tape it down and draw around it carefully with a pencil.

3

Cut out the mask. Ask for help with the holes. Decorate the mask so it looks the way you want it to.

4

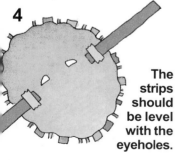

The strips should be level with the eyeholes.

Cut two cardboard strips 30cm (12in) long, 2cm (1in) wide. Tape them to the back of the mask like this.

5

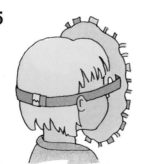

Overlap the strips around your head. Tape them together at the right length to hold the mask on.

Yarn and strips of paper glued on as a mane.

This queen mask has yellow yarn hair and gumdrop jewels.

Out and about

Drawings are all around you wherever you go. See how many different drawing styles you can find on everyday things.

Look for drawings on boxes and wrappings.

Pictures in books are called illustrations.

You can find cartoons in comics and newspapers.

Even a map is a kind of drawing.

Cartoons on television are made up of lots of drawings, like the flick books on page 25.

Keeping a sketchbook

A sketchbook is perfect for drawing in when you go out. You can also cut out other drawings and glue them in.

A book with plain pages and a hard cover is best. You can buy one at a card shop or art store.

Try drawing things that catch your eye, wherever you are. Take your sketchbook on holiday or on a walk.

You could draw flowers or trees.

You could draw whole buildings, or just look at one detail.

Glue drawings from old magazines and boxes into your book.

If you can't cut a picture out, you could try copying it.

Going to galleries

Art galleries are buildings where pictures are displayed for people to see. Many large towns have an art gallery, and it is often free to go in. If you go to a gallery, look out for drawings.

Galleries often sell postcards with their pictures on them.

Take your sketchbook and copy some of the pictures you like.

Some artists do small drawings before they do a painting. Sometimes you can see these next to paintings.

Artists and their styles

These drawings are done in the styles of some famous artists. You might see their drawings in a gallery.

Leonardo da Vinci (1452-1519) was an artist, scientist and inventor. He did detailed drawings of people, animals and machines.

Henri Matisse (1869-1954) experimented with bold lines in bright shades. He often drew with a brush and ink or paint.

Henry Moore (1898-1986) did rounded drawings of people and animals. He made sculptures and statues in the same style.

Paul Klee (1879-1940) drew and painted many buildings and landscapes. He liked to use patterns made up of lots of simple shapes.

M.C. Escher (1898-1970) is famous for his clever pencil drawings of animals, birds and other shapes that fit together.

Index

With special thanks to Jessica Roberts.

Photo of ducks on page 14: ©Pal Hermansen/Tony Stone Images.

First published in 1996 by Usborne Publishing Ltd, Usborne House, 83-85 Saffron Hill, London EC1N 8RT, England.
Copyright © 1996 Usborne Publishing Ltd.
First published in America March 1997.

Printed in Belgium.